SWEET BETSY FROM PIKE

VERSES SELECTED AND ILLUSTRATED BY

GLEN ROUNDS

Sweet Betsy, that inimitable "Pike County Rose," and her faithful lover Ike, whose exploits live on in one of America's most popular folk songs, have at last been rendered justice at the hands of Glen Rounds in a picture-book version of the song that is a laughter-filled delight from first page to last. No pretty cardboard characters are Mr. Rounds's Betsy and Ike. Betsy is the rough-tough pioneer woman, hell bent for leather and gold in California, who can shoot Indians from beneath a covered wagon or trip the light fantastic with the hoariest of miners. Big Ike, as Mr. Rounds has drawn him, is a masterpiece of foolhardy fidelity, lumbering and lovable, true to his Betsy until the bitter end. Their hardships and triumphs are faultlessly recorded in a book for all ages to enjoy and to return to time and again. A simple piano arrangement of the song is included.

SWEET BETSY FROM PIKE

CLAIM
756

A GOLDEN GATE JUNIOR BOOK
ℚ Childrens Press, Chicago

SWEET BETSY FROM PIKE

VERSES SELECTED AND ILLUSTRATED BY

GLEN ROUNDS

Library of Congress Cataloging in Publication Data

Rounds, Glen, 1906-
    Sweet Betsy from Pike.

    SUMMARY: Betsy and Ike, from Pike, endure the
hardships of the trip west during the California gold rush.
Based on the folk song.
    "A Golden Gate junior book."
    1.   Folk songs-US 2. North Carolina Collection
    I.   Title.
PZ8.3.R78Sw   [E]   72-94228   NC
ISBN 0-516-08855-6   J 184.406

SWEET BETSY
FROM PIKE

Oh, don't you remember Sweet Betsy from Pike
Who crossed the big mountains with her lover, Ike,

With two yoke of cattle, a large yellow dog,
A tall Shanghai rooster and one spotted hog?

One evening quite early they camped on the Platte—

'Twas nearby the road, on a green shady flat;

Where Betsy, quite tired, lay down to respose,
While Ike gazed with wonder on his Pike County rose.

They soon reached the desert, where Betsy gave out.
And down on the ground she lay rolling about

While Ike with great tears looked on in surprise,
Saying, "Betsy, get up, you'll get sand in your eyes!"

Sweet Betsy got up, in a great deal of pain,

And vowed she'd go back to Pike County again.

"Don't leave me," cried Ike, then they shyly embraced
And she traveled on West with his arm round her waist.

They stopped at Green River to inquire the way,
And a Preacher Man asked Sweet Betsy to stay.

But Betsy got frightened and ran like a deer
While Preacher stood pawing the dust like a steer.

Their wagon broke down with a terrible crash

And out on the prairie rolled all kinds of trash—

A few little baby clothes, done up with care—

'Twas rather suspicious, though all on the square.

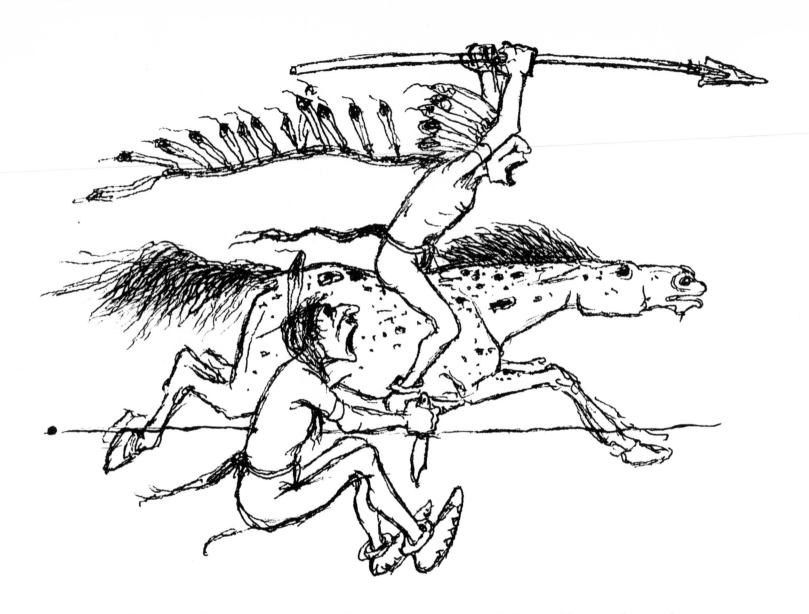

The Indians came down in a wild yelling horde
And Betsy was skeered they'd scalp her adored.

Behind the front wagon wheel Betsy did crawl
And there she fought Indians with musket and ball.

The Shanghai ran off and the cattle all died,
The last bits of bacon and corn meal were fried.

Poor Ike got discouraged and Betsy got mad—
The dog wagged his tail and looked wonderfully sad.

They limped through the sagebrush, dreaming of riches
Out there in that country where gold lay in ditches.

One morning they climbed up a high rocky hill
And looked down with wonder at old Placerville.

They'd swum the wide rivers and climbed the tall peaks
And camped on the prairie for weeks upon weeks,

With starvation and cholera and hard work and slaughter,
But they'd reached California over hell and high water.

Big Ike and Sweet Betsy attended a dance

Where Ike wore a pair of old Pike County pants.

Sweet Betsy was covered with ribbons and rings—
Quoth Ike, "You're an angel, but where are your wings?"

A miner said, "Betsy, will you dance with me?"
"I will, old Hoss, if you don't make too free.

But don't dance me hard—do you want to know why?
I'm full up to the brim with strong alkali!"

Big Ike and Sweet Betsy got married, of course,
And in time they'd bought them a broken down horse

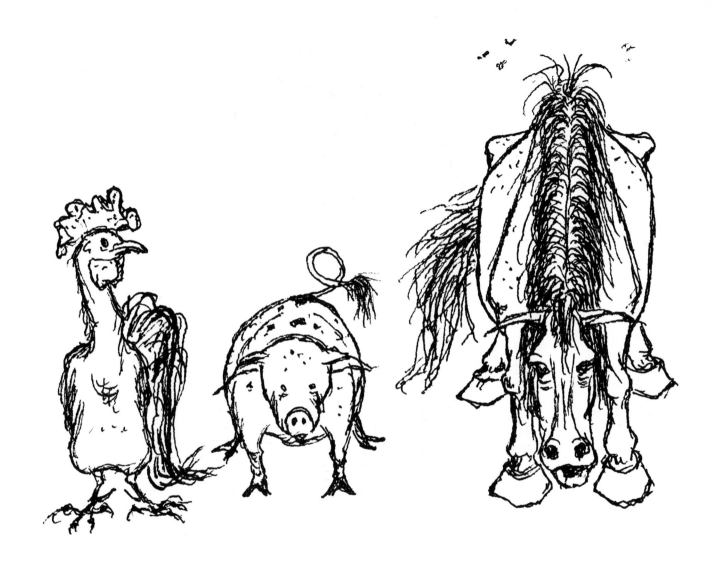

And another tall rooster, plus one spotted hog,

Which made a nice family, with the old yellow dog.

But gold grew scarce and they ran out of money.

"Let's go home," said Ike to his Pike County honey.

"Go home by yourself," said she, getting mad,
While the dog wagged his tail and looked wonderfully sad.

"Only leave me the hog to stay here in your place—
Whenever I see him I'll think of your face!"

So Ike started off, but he hadn't gone far

When his horse choked to death on a five-cent cigar.

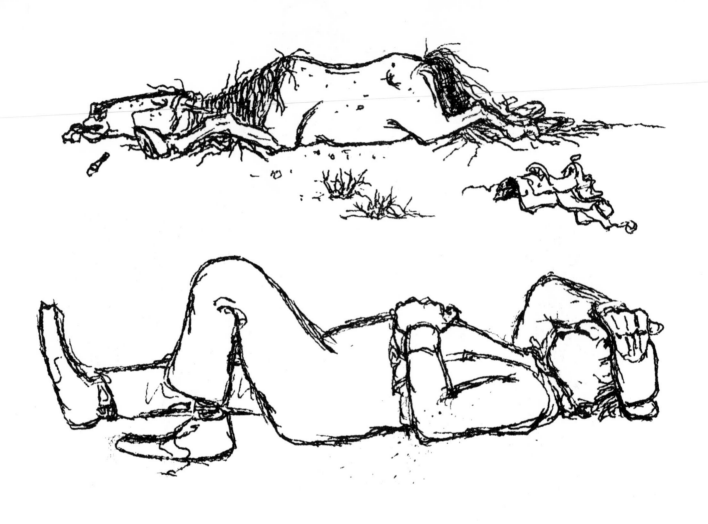

Poor Ike lay down in the sand, broken-hearted
To think that he and that old horse had parted.

Then along came Betsy with a cart and an ox,
Said she, "Our poor hog is now sick with the pox."

"All the good doctors are still back in Pike,
So let's hurry back there, good husband Ike."

He climbed aboard and he didn't look sad,
While the dog wagged his tail and looked wonderfully glad.

Sweet Betsy From Pike

Arranged by Patty Zeitlin

SWEET BETSY FROM PIKE

Oh don't you remember Sweet Betsy from Pike
Who crossed the big mountains with her lover, Ike,
With two yoke of cattle, a large yellow dog,
A tall Shanghai rooster and one spotted hog?

One evening quite early they camped on the Platte—
'Twas nearby the road, on a green shady flat;
Where Betsy, quite tired, lay down to repose,
While Ike gazed with wonder on his Pike County rose.

They soon reached the desert, where Betsy gave out,
And down on the ground she lay rolling about
While Ike with great tears looked on in surprise,
Saying, "Betsy, get up, you'll get sand in your eyes!"

Sweet Betsy got up, in a great deal of pain,
And vowed she'd go back to Pike County again.
"Don't leave me," cried Ike, then they shyly embraced
And she traveled on West with his arm round her waist.

They stopped at Green River to inquire the way,
And a Preacher Man asked Sweet Betsy to stay.
But Betsy got frightened and ran like a deer
While Preacher stood pawing the dust like a steer.

Their wagon broke down with a terrible crash
And out on the prairie rolled all kinds of trash—
A few little baby clothes, done up with care—
'Twas rather suspicious, though all on the square.

The Indians came down in a wild yelling horde
And Betsy was skeered they'd scalp her adored.
Behind the front wagon wheel Betsy did crawl
And there she fought Indians with musket and ball.

The Shanghai ran off and the cattle all died,
The last bits of bacon and corn meal were fried.
Poor Ike got discouraged and Betsy got mad—
The dog wagged his tail and looked wonderfully sad.

They limped through the sagebrush, dreaming of riches
Out there in that country where gold lay in ditches.
One morning they climbed up a high rocky hill
And looked down with wonder at old Placerville.

They'd swum the wide rivers and climbed the tall peaks
And camped on the prairie for weeks upon weeks,
With starvation and cholera and hard work and slaughter,
But they'd reached California over hell and high water.

Big Ike and Sweet Betsy attended a dance
Where Ike wore a pair of old Pike County pants.
Sweet Betsy was covered with ribbons and rings—
Quoth Ike, "You're an angel, but where are your wings?"

A miner said, "Betsy, will you dance with me?"
"I will, old Hoss, if you don't make too free.
But don't dance me hard—do you want to know why?
I'm full up to the brim with strong alkali!"

Big Ike and Sweet Betsy got married, of course,
And in time they'd bought them a broken down horse
And another tall rooster, plus one spotted hog,
Which made a nice family, with the old yellow dog.

But gold grew scarce and they ran out of money.
"Let's go home," said Ike to his Pike County honey.
"Go home by yourself," said she, getting mad,
While the dog wagged his tail and looked wonderfully sad.

"Only leave me the hog to stay here in your place—
Whenever I see him I'll think of your face!"
So Ike started off, but he hadn't gone far
When his horse choked to death on a five-cent cigar.

Poor Ike lay down in the sand, broken-hearted
To think that he and that old horse had parted.
Then along came Betsy with a cart and an ox,
Said she, "Our poor hog is now sick with the pox."

"All the good doctors are still back in Pike,
So let's hurry back there, good husband Ike."
He climbed aboard and he didn't look sad,
While the dog wagged his tail and looked wonderfully glad.

Refrain

Good-bye, Pike County—farewell for awhile—
We'll come back again when we've panned out our pile.

Last refrain

Good-bye, California—farewell for awhile—
We'll come back one day to replenish our pile.